Lovingly Presented to

_____

On _____

From _____

Mother,

" 'Many women do noble things,
but you surpass them all.' "

PROVERBS 31:29 NIV

$\mathcal{M}$others make a home a garden place
where seeds of hope and faith
are planted in young hearts–
where light, warmth, and
nourishment flourish–
where family roots grow strong
in the soil of love.

The love in children's hearts,
the values they cherish,
the joys they share,
the blessings they possess–
are all homemade.

I Remember Mother

As I remember special times
of family, home, and you–
all the happy things we shared
and all the love we knew–
my heart is warmed with good things
of what we shared back then.
How precious are the memories
that bring you close again!

I can't say you're
the ideal mother–
you surpassed that
long ago!

If motherhood were a recipe,

you'd be the main ingredient...

If it were a sporting activity,

you'd be the main event.

If it were a fabric,

you'd be a special blend...

If it were a novel,

You'd be the happy end!

*W*hen God made mothers,

He formed within them

the qualities of His own nature...

a ceaseless love, a watchful eye,

a caring touch, a serving spirit,

a protecting hand,

and a giving heart.

*Children receive so much
from their mother's
heart and hands,
because she gives
so freely.*

Recipe for Mother

First, take faith and kindness,
Then add joy and love.
Mix well with understanding–
Blend blessings from above.
Next, add lots of patience–
Bake with prayer and cheer,
And you will have the making
Of the mother I hold dear.

A mother is a giver,

and what sets her apart,

is that she gives her very best

for she gives

from her heart.

*M*any people have said to me,
"What a pity you had such a big family
to raise. Think of the novels and the
short stories and the poems you never had
time to write because of that." And I looked
at my children and I said, "These are my
poems. These are my short stories."

−OLGA MASTERS

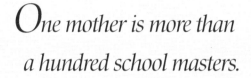

One mother is more than a hundred school masters.

–G. WORDSWORTH

"*By* wisdom a house is built,
and through understanding it is established;
through knowledge its rooms are filled
with rare and beautiful treasures."

PROVERBS 24:3, 4 NIV

"...*A* woman who fears the Lord
is to be praised."

PROVERBS 31:30 NIV

A mother is praised for the treasures
her children find within her–precious jewels
of the soul and spirit. These are the riches
that only love can give and only the
heart can understand.

⌘

A mother's building blocks are
caring eyes, a listening ear, an understanding
smile, and hugs that warm the inside.

"*Glad to find you so merry, my girls,*" *said a cheery voice at the door, and actors and audience turned to welcome a tall, motherly lady, with a 'can-I-help-you' look about her which was truly delightful. She was not elegantly dressed, but a noble-looking woman, and the girls thought the gray cloak and unfashionable bonnet covered the most splendid mother in the world.*

–From Louisa May Alcott's *Little Women*, the coming home of Mrs. Marsh just as her daughters were finishing a play rehearsal.

The rivers of blessings that flow
from a mother's heart to her children
broaden and deepen with time,
creating an ocean of influence,
love, and cherished memories.

Children are often

in a mother's thoughts

because they are always

in her heart.

*T*here is no gift like love...

*t*here is no place like home...

*t*here is no mom like you!

A mother is the best "school teacher"

a child will ever have. She teaches

by word and example...in the early morning

and late at night...when it is convenient

and inconvenient.

*S*he is the kind of teacher who knows

each child by heart.

No man is poor who has had a godly mother.

–ABRAHAM LINCOLN

When a child is praised, a mother is honored.

*No one has a mother
who is priceless...
she is worth far more
than that!*

∽

Into a precious vessel
God pours tenderness and love,
An understanding heart,
and all the joy a child dreams of...
He gives her His compassion
and a kindness like no other
Then wraps her in His quiet strength
and gently calls her "Mother."

—BONNIE JENSON

"*She openeth her mouth
with wisdom; and in her tongue
is the law of kindness.*"

PROVERBS 31:26 KJV

*There is no influence so powerful
as that of the mother.*

—SARAH JOSEPHA HALE

Mother–
teacher, helper, nurse,
giver, companion, encourager,
advisor, counselor, guide,
nurturer, and friend.

There is no velvet so soft
as a mother's lap...
no rose so sweet
as a mother's cheek...
no music so charming
as a mother's voice.
—BISHOP NEWMAN

Take the daughter of a good mother.
—FULLER

Rafaelle, the painter, tried again and again, for years, painting over and over that simple subject–a mother and her babe–and could not satisfy himself. Each of his paintings is most beautiful, each in a different way; and yet none of them is perfect. There is more beauty in that simple, every-day sight than he or any man could express by his pencil and his colors.

–CHARLES KINGSLEY

$\mathcal{N}$obody knows of the work it makes
To keep the home together:
$\mathcal{N}$obody knows of the steps it takes,
$\mathcal{N}$obody knows–but mother.
$\mathcal{N}$obody kneels at the throne above
To thank the $\mathcal{H}$eavenly $\mathcal{F}$ather
$\mathcal{F}$or that sweetest gift–a mother's love,
$\mathcal{N}$obody can–but mother.

–H. C. DODGE

*W*e never know the love of the parent till we become parents ourselves. When we first bend over the cradle of our own child, God throws back the temple door, and reveals to us the sacredness and mystery of a mother's love.

–HENRY WARD BEECHER

*No language can express the power,
and beauty, and heroism, and majesty
of a mother's love. It shrinks not
where man cowers, and grows stronger
where man faints, and over the wastes
of worldly fortune sends the radiance
of its quenchless fidelity like
a star in heaven.*

—CHAPIN

It has been said that the sweetest words in our language are "Mother, Home, and Heaven;" and one might almost say the word "home" included them all; for who can think of home without remembering the gentle mother who sanctified it by her presence? And is not home the dearest name for heaven? We think of that better land as a home where brightness will never end in night. Oh, then, may our homes on earth be the centers of all our joys; may they be as green spots in the desert, to which we can retire when weary of the cares and perplexities of life, and drink the clear waters of a love which we know to be sincere and always unfailing.

–*Saturday Evening Post* late 1800's issue

*"Love...always protects, always trusts,
always hopes, always perseveres.
Love never fails...."*

I CORINTHIANS 13:6-8 NIV

*Mother, life's greatest treasures can't outdo
a loving kiss and hug from you.*

*O*bserve how soon, and to what a degree,
a mother's influence begins to operate!
Her first ministration for her infant is to
enter, as it were, the valley of the shadow
of death, and win its life at the peril of her
own! How different must an affection
thus formed, be from all others.

—SIGOURNEY

A mother's arms are made of tenderness,
and children sleep soundly in them.

–Victor Hugo

*A*ll that I am or hope to be,
I owe to my mother.

–Abraham Lincoln

I could never say it enough,

show it enough,

give it enough...

the love that is

in my heart for you,

Mother.

*T*here is one in the world who feels for him who is sad,
a keener pang than he feels for himself; there is one
to whom reflected joy is better than that which comes
direct; there is one who rejoices in another's honor more
than in any which is one's own; there is one on whom
another's transcendent excellence sheds no beam but that
of delight; there is one who hides another's deformities
more faithfully than one's own; there is one who loses all
sense of self in the sentiment of kindness, tenderness and
devotion to another; that one is mother.

—WASHINGTON IRVING

Mother,

" 'The Lord bless you and keep you;
the Lord make His face shine upon you
and be gracious to you;
the Lord turn His face toward you
and give you peace.' "

NUMBERS 6:24-26 NIV